CLOSER LOOK AT

SHARKS, PIRANHAS,

EELS AND OTHER FISH

Joyce Pope

Franklin Watts

LONDON ● SYDNEY

An Aladdin Book

© Aladdin Books Ltd 1997
Designed and produced by
Aladdin Books Ltd
28 Percy Street
London W1P 0LD

First published in Great Britain
in 1997 by
Franklin Watts
96 Leonard Street
London EC2A 4RH

A catalogue record for this book is available from the
British Library.

ISBN: 0 7496 2828 6

Editor
Michael Flaherty

Designer
Gary Edgar-Hyde

Picture Research
Brooks Krikler Research

Front cover illustration
Gary Edgar-Hyde

Illustrators
David Burroughs, Roy Coombs
Mick Loates, Mike Saunders
Ian Thompson, Norman Weaver

Certain illustrations have appeared in
earlier books created by Aladdin Books.

The consultant, Sue Thornton, is an Honours graduate
in Zoology and a qualified vet. She worked as Clinical
Veterinarian with stranded marine mammals at the
Marine Mammal Center in California, USA. She is
now responsible for the clinical care of all animals at
the Zoological Society of London, including those in
the aquarium.

Printed in Belgium

CONTENTS

4. Introduction
6. Fishes great and small
8. How fish swim
10. Fish teeth and food
12. Sharks
14. Shark relatives
16. Fish families
18. Migrating fishes
20. Fishes out of water
22. Coral reef fishes
24. Deep-sea fishes
26. Unusual fishes
28. Fishes and people
30. Fascinating fish facts
31. Glossary
32. Index

INTRODUCTION

Imagine a world where you couldn't fall over, but you could drift up and down as if you were flying. A calm world, where there were few storms, and the weather was almost the same all through the year. A twilight world, where you could not see but often had to feel for food or friends or foes. A noisy world, where sounds could carry for hundreds of kilometres and where sound could be used as a weapon to kill. This is not an invented place, but the world of water, the world of fishes.

About 25,000 different kinds of fish live in the oceans, lakes and rivers of the world. Most are streamlined creatures. Only a few, like plaice or seahorses, are other shapes. These fishes are inactive or swim slowly. The biggest fishes all live in the open sea. Tiny fishes mostly live in small spaces in coral reefs or in ponds and streams.

Tiddlers

The tiniest fish is the dwarf goby. Males are smaller than females and measure less than a centimetre long. They live only in one lake in Luzon in the Philippines. These fish have no coloured scales and are almost transparent. Another goby, almost as small, used to be used as food in Luzon. The fishes were dried and pressed into a block. It took about 70,000 to make a block weighing 450 gm (1 lb).

FISHES GREAT

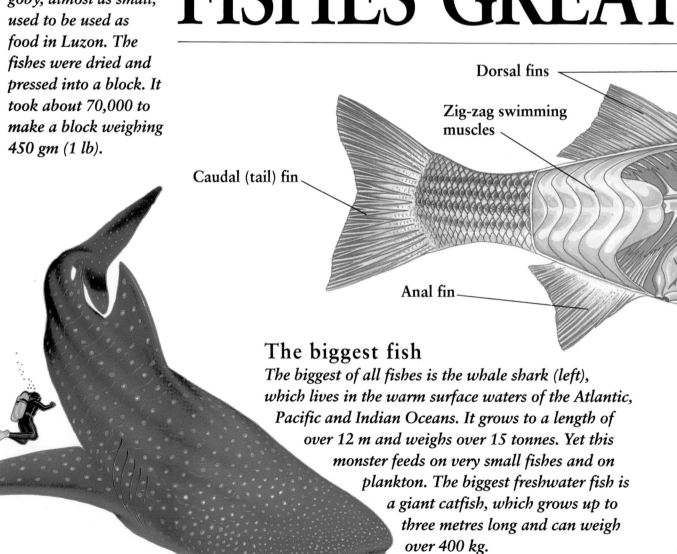

Dorsal fins

Zig-zag swimming muscles

Caudal (tail) fin

Anal fin

The biggest fish

The biggest of all fishes is the whale shark (left), which lives in the warm surface waters of the Atlantic, Pacific and Indian Oceans. It grows to a length of over 12 m and weighs over 15 tonnes. Yet this monster feeds on very small fishes and on plankton. The biggest freshwater fish is a giant catfish, which grows up to three metres long and can weigh over 400 kg.

ON CLOSER INSPECTION – *Lampreys*

Lampreys (right) and hagfishes look like eels, but they are very different. Their skin has no scales. Inside their bodies, they have no bones, but a stiff, gristly rod for support. They have no jaws, but a mouth that acts like a sucker with horny teeth to grind at food.

AND SMALL

Vertebrae (bones of the back)

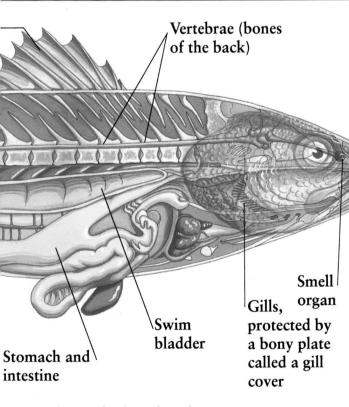

Stomach and intestine

Swim bladder

Gills, protected by a bony plate called a gill cover

Smell organ

Inside a fish's body
Fishes (except for those in the shark family) have a skeleton of true bone inside their bodies and are called bony fishes. They have similar gills, liver and heart regardless of their shape.

Shark denticles

TILES OR SANDPAPER?
The skin of sharks and their relatives – rays and skates – have tiny, hard tooth-like structures, called dermal denticles (above), embedded in their skin. Most other fishes are protected by small, thin plates of bone, called scales (below), that are set like overlapping roof tiles in their skin.

Overlapping, bony fish scales

A person or a fish swimming has to push through the water, which is 800 times as dense as air. When we swim, some of our energy is used to hold us up. Fishes do not waste energy like this. Most have a gas-filled swim bladder inside them, which works like a lifebuoy, so a fish can keep at a constant depth without any effort.

Gill propulsion

Watch a fish in a tank. Part of the time, it will hang motionless in the water. Every now and then it will back-paddle with its fins. This is so that it can keep in the same position, for it is propelled forwards by the water that passes out of its gill slits.

Direction of water flow

Gill filaments supported on the gill arch

Gill arch

Gills

Fishes breathe, using oxygen that is dissolved in water. They do this with their gills. A fish takes water into its mouth. It then drives the water out over its gills. As it does so, oxygen passes into the blood that flows just below the delicate skin of the gill filaments (above). At the same time, a waste gas, called carbon dioxide, passes from the blood into the water and is pumped out of the fish's gills.

HOW FISH

The cruising speed of the great white shark (above) is about 3 km/h. To catch prey, it can speed up to 25 km/h for short distances.

Fishes do not live in a silent world, for water carries sound very well and so fishes communicate with each other. They cannot talk, but many species have a special muscle that twangs against the swim bladder, so they have a kind of drum language.

SWIM

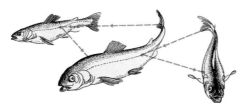

On its sides a fish has a series pressure-sensitive cells called the lateral line system (left). Even though the water is dark or murky, the fish is aware of anything moving nearby.

SWIMMING

As it swims, a fish shortens the zig-zag-shaped muscles on its sides, first on one side, then on the other. It curves its body left and right and, helped by its tail, pushes itself through the water. Its fins are used for balancing, steering and braking and only rarely for active forward movement.

Most of the forward thrust in fast-swimming fishes, such as tuna, comes from their tails, with little movement in the body. They have forked or crescent-shaped tails and curved pectoral (side) fins. Slow-swimming fish, such as bowfins, have more rounded tails and fins.

Pitch

Roll

Yaw

The fins on a fish's back and belly are stabilisers. They can be used to make (or prevent) it tilt, or pitch, roll sideways and swing from side to side, or yaw (above).

Dogfish swimming

These diagrams (left) show the way that a small shark, called a dogfish, swings its body into curves as it swims. The head hardly moves from the direction in which it is travelling. The greatest movement is in the powerful tail, which thrusts the water away behind it, pushing the fish forwards.

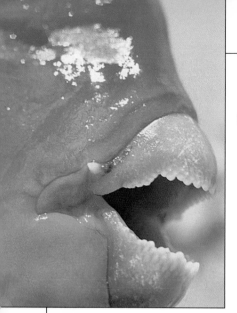

The majority of fishes feed on flesh. Many have strong jaws and a lot of teeth. They often specialise in a certain kind of food and their teeth have evolved to meet their needs. Tiny animals feed on microscopic plankton. These in turn are eaten by larger fish and other creatures. Some freshwater fishes feed on plants, but these are few in number.

FISH TEETH

Beaked fishes

Parrot fishes (above) have some of the strongest teeth in the fish world. They feed on coral, which they bite off with the big teeth in the front of their mouths. They grind up this stony food and digest the small organisms living in and on it.

Freshwater hunter

Pike (below) live in fresh water. They are fearsome hunters. In the first few months of life, they feed on small creatures, but as they grow they move on to larger fishes and even water birds. They have many sharp, backward-pointing teeth, which prevent prey from escaping their grasp.

SHARK'S TEETH

A shark's aggressive way of life means that its teeth often wear down or break off. The shark does not need to worry, for it always has many others in reserve. These grow up inside the jaw, and push to the front of the mouth, constantly replacing the older worn, broken or missing teeth. So the shark always has a battery of sharp, new teeth to use.

Gill rakers of filter feeders sift food from the water.

ON CLOSER INSPECTION
– Moray eel

Moray eels usually live in crevices in rocks or coral reefs. All that can be seen of them is their heads, armed with needle-sharp teeth. When small, they feed on shrimps and little fish. As they grow bigger they become fierce hunters, feeding on larger creatures.

AND FOOD

BASKING SHARKS

The basking shark is the second largest fish in the oceans, growing to a length of 11 m, yet its teeth are so tiny that its jaws look as if they are lined with sandpaper. The reason is that it feeds only on tiny plankton that it strains from the water with special comb-like structures on its gills, called gill rakers.

Teeth exposed and in use

Teeth growing in jaw

Jaw cartilage

Nibblers

Butterfly fishes (right) feed on coral polyps. They use the tiny, pointed teeth at the end of their long jaws to nibble their soft prey from its stony home.

There are over 350 different sorts of shark. All of them are flesh-eaters. Sharks are very different from other sorts of fish. Their skeletons are not made of bone, but of a softer, gristly stuff, called cartilage. Their gills are not protected by gill covers, but lie as open slits behind the head.

Sand tiger shark

The ragged teeth of the three-metre-long sand tiger shark make it look fierce, but it is usually harmless to people unless it is defending itself.

The spots on its snout (above) are part of a sensitive detection system that picks up tiny electric currents made by the muscle movements of small fishes and squid that are its usual prey.

SHARKS

GREAT WHITE SHARK

The great white shark (below) normally hunts large animals like tuna, sea lions and also other sharks. This shark is probably the most feared of all fishes, for it has even attacked fishing boats and many people who have ventured into the waters where it lives. Nobody knows why it should do this, for people are not its natural food. But humans have taken their revenge and hunted the great white shark. In many places, it is now so rare that it is protected by law.

The great white shark and its relative, the mako shark, are warm-blooded, like mammals, birds and a few other fast-swimming fishes, such as tuna. Being able to maintain a warmer body temperature allows for faster movement when needed, a necessity for a successful predator.

ON CLOSER INSPECTION
– The shark's friend

On the top of its head a remora (right) has a sucker disc to attach itself to larger animals such as sharks. The remoras nibble parasites from the shark's skin and help clear up the afterbirth when shark pups are born.

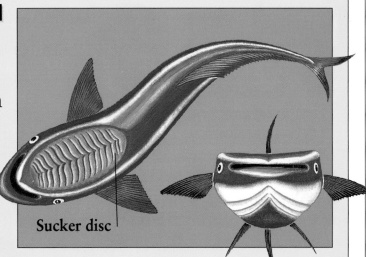

Sucker disc

SWIMMER'S BUILD

Sharks do not have a swim bladder, but their livers are rich in oil, which gives them added buoyancy. Most of them cannot rest without sinking. Shark species that live in open waters (right) must swim all of their lives and they are streamlined to do this efficiently. The pectoral fins are not as moveable as those of bony fish. They help to give sharks lift as they swim. The fast swimmers, like the white and the tiger sharks, have tail lobes of nearly equal size.

The great white shark

The whaler shark

The tiger shark

The hammerhead shark

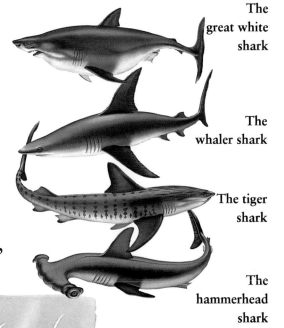

Hammerheads

These strangely shaped sharks (above and left) usually hunt at night. By day they often swim together in large schools. In such groups there are about four females to each male. They may be courtship parties, though they have never been seen mating.

Electric Ray

The electric ray (below) has developed the ability to give off bursts of electricity. Its electric organs are just behind its head and gills. It uses the electricity to stun the fishes it feeds on and for defence. Scientists are unsure how the ray generates the electricity.

Skates and rays are fishes that do not look a bit like sharks, but they are in fact similar in many ways and are closely related. Like sharks they have skeletons of cartilage, unprotected gill slits and dermal denticles. Their flat shape is an adaptation to life on the sea bed, where most of them prey on hard-shelled creatures, such as clams or crabs.

SHARK

MANTA RAY

The manta ray looks like other rays but it has taken to living in the surface waters of tropical seas. It grows to an enormous size of more than 6 m across, feeding on a rich diet of microscopic animals and plants called plankton. It guides the minute creatures into its mouth with two hand-like fins and strains them from the water through filters attached to its gills. This is why it is called a filter feeder. In spite of its enormous size, it is completely harmless to humans.

Rays cannot escape quickly if they are discovered by an enemy. Many of them can defend themselves with stings set on their tails. These are saw-edged spines connected to poison glands. If anything attacks the fish, it lashes its tail until it stings the predator.

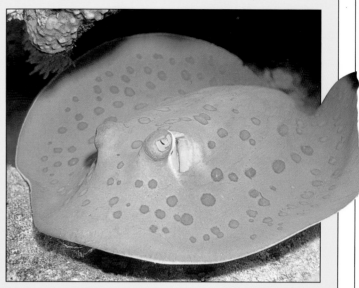

RELATIVES

RAYS SWIMMING

Skates and rays have broad, flat bodies. The width of their bodies is formed from their large fins. Their tails are long and narrow and of no use for swimming, so unlike almost all other fishes, they use their big pectoral (side) fins for locomotion (below). It is a most graceful way of swimming, for the rays look as if they are flying through the water as they raise and lower their huge, flexible wing-like fins.

The common skate (right) can grow up to two metres wide. It preys on fish including other rays.

Life on the bottom

Many rays and skates are almost completely camouflaged as they lie buried in the surface of the sand. Their gills are on the underside of their bodies so they breathe by taking in clean water through holes called spiracles, that lie on the top of their bodies behind their eyes.

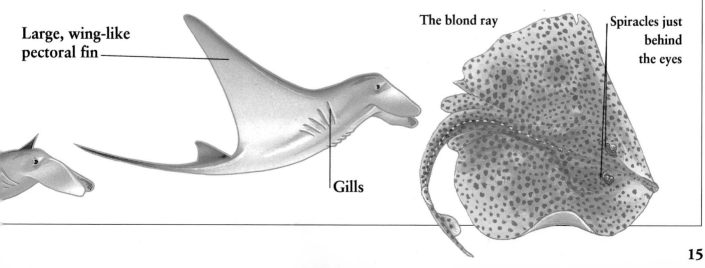

Large, wing-like pectoral fin

Gills

The blond ray

Spiracles just behind the eyes

ost fishes do not have a family life as we understand it. Females lay far too many eggs to care for the young individually. In many sea fishes, each egg contains a tiny drop of oil, which helps it to float. In their early days, the young of such huge families form part of the plankton. Most are eaten by other sea creatures and few survive to become adults.

FISH

Nesting fish

The male stickleback plays the nursemaid to his family. He builds a nest from waterweed (above). After a female lays her eggs, he drives her off. He guards the nest and then the babies for about two weeks after they hatch.

Sockeye salmon

Sockeye salmon (below) return to the rivers in which they were born in order to spawn. After egg laying, the fish die.

SEAHORSE FATHERS

After mating, a female seahorse pushes her eggs into a pouch on her mate's belly. The eggs hatch and the young grow in safety in the pouch until eventually the male gives birth (right). He watches over the young for a short time, though they are not able to return to the pouch for protection.

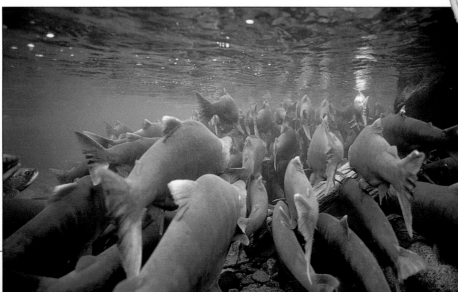

ON CLOSER INSPECTION – *Egg production*

The larger the bony fish, the more eggs she is likely to produce. A female sunfish (right), which can grow to 3.5 m long, can produce 30 million eggs at each spawning – far more than any other fish.

FAMILIES

Mouth nursery

Cichlid fishes (below) are known as 'mouth brooders'. The females of many kinds make their mouths a nursery to hold their eggs and, later, their young. When the mother needs to feed, she is careful to spit the babies out first!

SHARKS

Sharks usually have small families. In some, such as the lemon shark (below), the eggs hatch inside the mother's body. The babies are nourished inside the mother's body before being born alive. Others, like the dogfish, lay eggs in tough, horny cases, called mermaid's purses, where they develop for about a year into strong young fishes able to look after themselves.

Cat shark egg case

Spiral egg case of a Port Jackson shark

Lemon shark giving birth to live young

Shape changing
The tiny creature that hatches from an eel's egg is very different from the snake-shaped adults. It looks like a tiny, transparent leaf. It begins its journey from the Sargasso Sea to the rivers where its parents lived. After about three years, it is as big as a pencil and is ready to enter a river in which it will grow.

Fishes of many species gather into large groups to lay eggs, or spawn. Sometimes they make long journeys to spawn in places where the water is shallow or warm, or where there will be plenty of food for the baby fish when they hatch. The greatest migrations are made by salmon and eels, which also cope with the change between salt and fresh water.

MIGRATING

1
2
3
4

1 Eel larva at two months, 25 mm long
2 Larva at eight months, 45 mm long
3 Larva at 18 months, 75 mm long
4 Elver at three years, 65 mm long

The numbers on the map (below) correspond with the stages of development of the eel larvae (above) as they travel across the Atlantic Ocean to freshwater rivers.

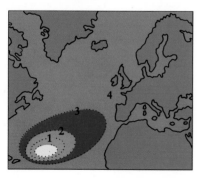

THE EEL'S LIFE HISTORY
After a journey from the Sargasso Sea lasting three years to Europe or one year to North America, young eels become small, transparent versions of their parents as they enter freshwater rivers. They turn yellow as they feed. As yellow eels (right), they grow to adulthood in seven to ten years. When mature, they turn silver. As silver eels (right), they return to the sea to spawn before dying.

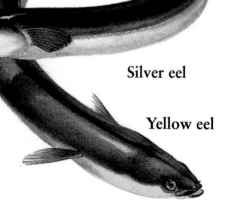

Silver eel

Yellow eel

ON CLOSER INSPECTION
– *The salmon's struggle*

Salmon return from the sea to the rivers in which they were spawned to lay their eggs. They must reach cool, clear, fast-running water for their eggs to hatch. They often have to cross rapids and leap falls in journeys that may take them over 2,000 km upstream.

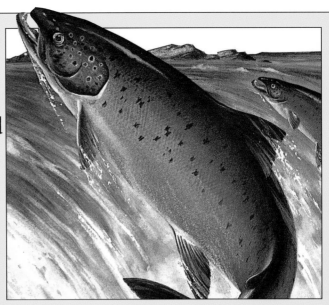

FISHES

SEASONAL MIGRATION

Many fishes make migrations less spectacular than the eel or the salmon. Tuna live in shoals and make seasonal migrations following fishes, including herring, that are their food. Herring migrate in the breeding season, from deep to shallow water, to spawn.

Herring

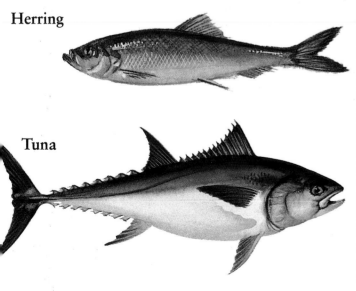

Tuna

SALMON LADDER

Humans have altered many salmon rivers, damming them to make reservoirs or to make hydroelectric power. Salmon cannot pass such obstacles, so often salmon ladders (below) are constructed. These provide a series of stepped pools that the fish can use to reach the upper streams.

If taken out of water, most fishes die quickly, but a few kinds can survive. Most of these live at the edge of the sea or in pools and swamps that are likely to dry up. They have developed ways of using oxygen from the air as well as taking it from the water with their gills.

FISHES OUT

Fishes in trees

Travellers to the East brought back stories of fishes called climbing perch. These fishes often move across dry land from one pond to another. They wriggle along, helped by their strong fins and by big spines on their gill covers. Often they are caught by birds, such as crows, which hide them in trees to be eaten later. People thought the fish climbed the trees, hence their name. Climbing perch will suffocate if kept entirely underwater.

Mythical animals

In the past, many people believed in strange fish-like creatures that could live partly at least out of water, like this sea devil (below), pictured by a 16th-century artist called Gessner.

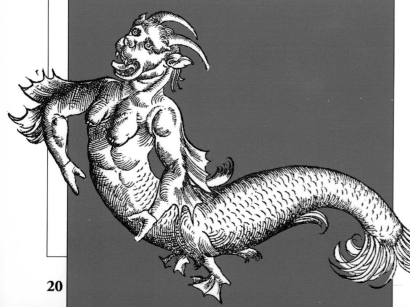

MUDSKIPPER

The mudskipper (above) lives in mangrove swamps and mud flats. At low tide, it moves about on the mud using its pectoral fins and tail. These help it to skip over the mud and escape enemies, which it sees with its large eyes. With enlarged gill chambers the mudskipper carries water for breathing, but it can also breathe air.

ON CLOSER INSPECTION
– *Gills and lungs*

Some fishes, such as loaches and some catfish (right), must swallow air to survive. Part of their intestine is swollen and acts as a lung, taking oxygen from the air and passing it directly into the bloodstream.

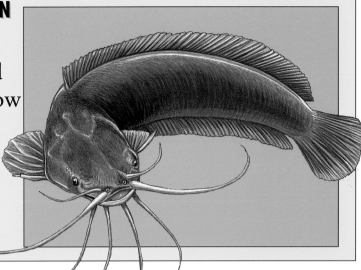

OF WATER

LUNGFISHES

Lungfishes live in Australia, Africa and South America. As their pools dry up, they survive by breathing air, using lungs connected to their swim bladder. Some bury themselves in mud (below), making a cocoon of slime that hardens. They then go into a state of sleep, called aestivation, and some survive for over two years until the next rains.

Gas space

Blood vessels

The lining of the lungfish's lungs (above) has a rich supply of blood vessels, in order to absorb oxygen from the gulped air.

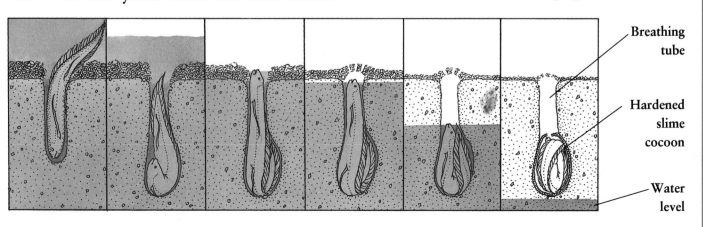

Breathing tube

Hardened slime cocoon

Water level

oral reefs are found in all shallow, warm seas. They are formed of the hard skeletons of tiny relatives of the sea anemone, called coral polyps. The surface of the reef is covered with living, growing polyps, which provide shelter for more kinds of fishes than are found in any other habitat. Many reef fishes have narrow bodies and can swim easily through the branching passages of their homes.

CORAL REEF

Deadly stone
Not all the fishes of a coral reef are brightly coloured. Some, such as the stonefish (above), are dull in colour to match dead coral, mud, stone or sand. They are almost impossible to see as they lie on the sea bed and wait for their prey. The stonefish has sharp spines on its back connected to glands that produce a strong poison. Stonefishes live in waters from the Red Sea to East Africa and across the Indian Ocean to Australia.

SEX CHANGE
Anthias (right) are found in reefs in the Red Sea and the Indian and Pacific Oceans. They normally live around one small area of coral, where they take shelter if they are frightened. The smaller fishes in a school are all females; the one larger fish with them is a male. If he dies, or is taken away, the most senior of the females grows larger, changes sex and takes his place.

ON CLOSER INSPECTION
– Blue-striped grunts

These are common fishes of the reefs of the West Indies. The young fish live in inshore waters. The adults, which, at about 46 cm in length, are larger than most kinds of reef fishes, and form small schools among the corals. As their name suggests, they make grunting sounds, in and out of water, by grinding throat teeth together.

FISHES

Each clown fish becomes accepted slowly by only one particular sea anemone. If the clown fish were to visit another sea anemone, it would be stung to death and eaten.

CLOWN FISH

Clown fishes (below left) have a special way of keeping safe. When in danger, they take refuge among the poisonous tentacles of large sea anemones. Each fish has one anemone that does not sting it. The anemone is rewarded for its tolerance. Any predator that is chasing the clown fish is caught by the anemone.

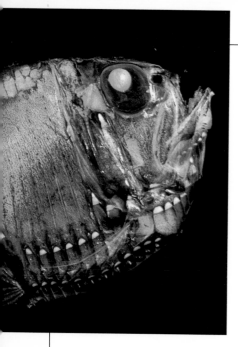

The average depth of the sea is about 2,500 metres. Much of it is cold and dark, with little food, for no green plants can grow there. Some of the strangest of all fishes live in this hostile environment. Most are small, with fragile bodies, but they have huge teeth to grab and hold infrequent meals, which may be larger than the hunters themselves.

DEEP-SEA

Luminous fishes

Many deep-sea fishes have light-producing organs on their bodies, like the hatchet fish (above). The lights can be flashed on and off for various reasons. In some species they may act as signals to keep fishes of the same kind together. In the breeding season, they may enable males and females to find each other. Sudden flashes of light may also help to startle predators.

DEVILS OF THE DEEP

Most deep-sea fishes are black in colour to match the darkness in which they live. Their eyes are able to pick up very faint glimmers of light from other creatures around them. Many have small light organs near their eyes so that they will not be blinded by an enemy that suddenly switches on its lights. The huge mouths, armed with many sharp, pointed teeth of species like photostomias and viperfishes mean that their prey seldom escapes them. These fish swim along in the darkness with their mouths gaping, ready to snap up anything that comes along.

Lantern fish

Viperfish

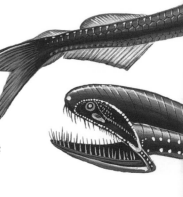

The diagram (right) shows three types of deep-sea fish that produce their own light. The viperfish and the photostomias both have huge, sharp teeth and are merciless hunters.

ON CLOSER INSPECTION
– *Tripod fish*

Many deep-sea fishes make journeys to upper layers of the sea, often at night, to feed, but the tripod fish remains on the sea bed at depths of over 3,000 metres. It balances itself on the tips of its hugely lengthened pectoral fins and the lower part of the tail fin and uses them rather like stilts to skip along over the soft mud.

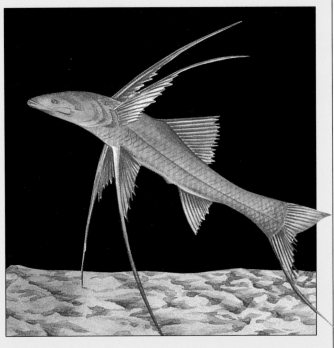

FISHES

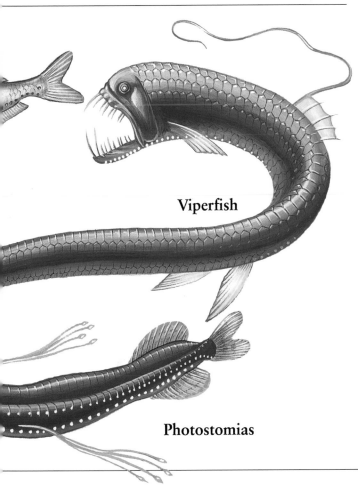

Viperfish

Photostomias

ANGLER FISH

There are many sorts of angler fish (below) in the deep sea. They lure their prey with a light on the end of a long, flexible spine on their heads, slowly drawn within reach of their huge jaws.

Some male angler fish are so small that they attach themselves to a mate and feed on her blood like a parasite. This overcomes the problems of males meeting females in the dark vastness of the oceans.

Archerfish

The archerfish (below) is so named because it can spit jets of water with great force up to 1.5 metres into the air to knock a fly off its perch. The unsuspecting prey drops into the water. Then the hungry fish grabs the struggling insect before it has time to escape. This skill does not come automatically, so young archerfish need a lot of target practice to improve their aim.

Fishes live almost everywhere that there is water, from the deepest oceans to the shallowest streams. They feed on almost everything edible, from the tiny to the huge, which they subdue by working as a group tearing with many teeth. They have many ways of escaping from their enemies. Some are speedy, some are camouflaged, some pretend a fierceness they do not possess.

UNUSUAL

ESCAPING FROM ENEMIES

There are two kinds of oceanic flying fish. Some have two 'wings' – enlarged pectoral fins – while others have four 'wings' – enlarged pectoral and pelvic fins. Flying fishes (below) are not the fastest fishes in the sea, but when they are frightened, they use their speed in a special way. Travelling at up to 30 km/h, they make a sudden leap and spread their huge fins. They do not flap their fins, but glide like paper darts, for distances of up to 400 metres and, lifted by the wind, sometimes at a height of over five metres. They cannot steer, but may dip the enlarged lower half of their tails into the water for further take-offs.

ON CLOSER INSPECTION
– *En garde!*

The swordfish charges into schools of fishes, slashing to either side with its sword-like upper jaw. It then eats the dead and injured fishes. Sometimes swordfishes hit small boats. The sword may drive up to half a metre into the wood and usually breaks as the creature struggles to escape.

FISHES

PIRANHA

There are several kinds of piranha (below), all of which live in the rivers of the Amazon Basin in South America. They have massive, powerful lower jaws with triangular, razor-sharp teeth. They hunt in shoals of up to several thousand and may attack any large animal that enters the water. About four species are dangerous to humans.

PORCUPINE

Porcupine fishes (above) are slow swimmers. Armoured with spines, they inflate themselves like balloons by swallowing water or air. Their spines stand out to make them an impossible mouthful for any predator.

ishes are often slimy and are not considered clever or cute like mammals or birds. Though people catch fishes, eat fish and sometimes keep them, in general we feel little warmth towards fishes. We have often polluted or destroyed their habitats. We catch and treat them in ways that have changed little since the days of our barbaric ancestors.

FISHES AND

Prehistoric art

Fish has been an important part of people's food since prehistoric times. Fish hooks made of bone have been found in the caves that were lived in by prehistoric people. One such hook may have been used to catch this fish (above), which was carved into a cave wall in Spain by somebody who lived there over 15,000 years ago. The tuna, the salmon and other fishes were not only valued as food by early people. People admired them for their beauty and their strength and hoped to gain some of this for themselves with their pictures and sculptures.

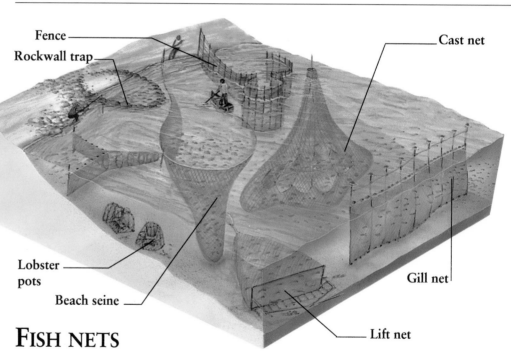

Fence
Rockwall trap
Cast net
Lobster pots
Beach seine
Gill net
Lift net

FISH NETS

Most of the fishes that we eat today are caught in nets (above). Some nets are like a wall of fine mesh, stretching for 20 km through the sea. Unfortunately, these nets also catch and drown creatures such as dolphins, turtles and sea birds. Conservationists are trying to find ways that will enable these animals to avoid the nets and also to control the use of small mesh nets that catch young fish.

On Closer Inspection
– Feeding sharks

A hundred years ago, many kinds of animals were killed ruthlessly for sport and for food. Now our attitude is changing. Lots of people enjoy watching animals. Some people on holiday get a thrill from watching and even feeding sharks.

PEOPLE

TRAWLERS AND FACTORY SHIPS

Other nets called trawl nets are dragged along the sea bed, often damaging fish nesting grounds and other sea animals. Fishes that are caught by big factory ships (above) are often gutted and frozen within hours of being caught. Fishes not used as food are killed unnecessarily and thrown back into the sea.

FISH FARM

Some fishes have been brought close to extinction by overfishing. This means more fish are caught than can be replaced through breeding. One way to improve matters is by farming fish. We do not know how to farm all species of fish, but some kinds, including some sea fishes such as salmon and turbot, can be farmed. Fish farms protect the fishes from predators and provide them with the nutrients they need.

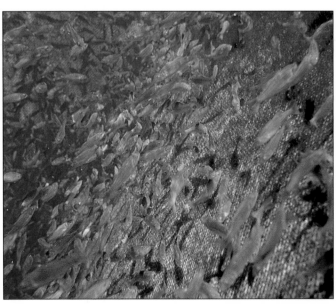

The Ozark cavefish of North America has become blind in its lightless world.

FANTASTIC FISH FACTS

In the total darkness of caves, the eyes of many fishes are small and sightless or have even disappeared. Such fishes (left) rely on a well-developed lateral line system.

The most abundant fish in the world is probably a small, deep-water fish called a bristlemouth. It is found in all the oceans except for the very coldest waters.

The fastest-swimming fish is the cosmopolitan sailfish, a relative of the swordfish. It has been recorded at a speed of 109 km/h over a short distance. Other fast-swimming fishes are marlins and the bluefin and the yellowfin tuna. Marlins, which can reach 80 km/h in short bursts, can keep up a speed nearly as high as this for long periods.

Fishes that have actually achieved powered flight are the South American freshwater hatchet fishes (below). They have a deep chest, like that of a bird, with powerful muscles. These muscles enable the fishes to flap their pectoral fins rapidly enough to give them the uplift needed for take-off and flight.

The longest bony fish in the world is the oarfish, which usually lives in the deep sea.

The oarfish can grow up to 10 m long. It has a slender body, so it weighs comparatively little.

Rediscovered in 1938, the coelacanth was thought to have died out 200 million years ago.

The rarest fish in the world is probably the Devil's Hole pupfish, which lives in one small pool, about 20 metres square, fed by a spring, in Nevada, U.S.A. It can survive in water temperatures up to 42°C. In the winter, about 200 fishes live in the pool; in the summer, the numbers rise to about 700.

The present-day coelacanths (above) are almost identical to fossils found in rocks 300 million years old. They have fleshy fins and their ancient relatives may have given rise to four-legged animals. They live in deep water (below 150 m) off the coast of the the Comoros Islands in the Indian Ocean.

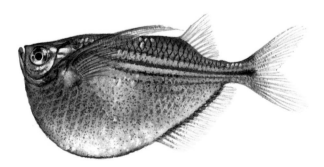

This hatchet fish can fly by flapping its fins.

Aestivation A state of inactivity, like hibernation, that occurs in some tropical animals (including fishes) in seasons too hot and dry for normal activity.

Carbon dioxide A gas that is a waste product of the living processes of animals.

Cartilage A stiff, gristly material that is part of the skeleton of animals with backbones, including ourselves. Sharks' skeletons are made entirely of cartilage, hardened in places by calcium minerals, but not of true bone.

Cold-blooded An animal that cannot regulate its own body temperature. Its temperature, and thus its activity, are controlled by the temperature of its surroundings.

Coral reef A rocky reef made of the hard, chalky skeletons of small corals creatures, which live in shallow tropical seas. Each coral creature is called a polyp.

Dermal denticles Enamel-covered, tooth-like structures set in the skin of sharks, skates and rays. Dermal denticles are mostly smaller than a pin's head.

Environment The place and conditions in which an animal lives.

Gills The breathing apparatus of fishes. The gills lie just behind the head of a fish. They look like pink feathers. Oxygen in the water passes through the gills into the fish's blood. Carbon dioxide passes out into the water at the same time.

Gill cover A big plate of bone that covers and protects the gills of bony fishes.

Gill raker A comb-like structure attached to the bones that support a fish's gills. Water goes through the gill rakers and tiny food particles are combed out and swallowed.

Lateral line system A series of pressure-sensitive spots along the side of a fish. The animal can feel the nearness of food or foes by changes in pressure of water on its sides.

Oxygen A gas taken out of the water by a fish's gills. It is needed for all the activities of life, such as moving, digestion and the build-up of food stores in the body.

Pectoral fin One of a pair of fins that lies behind a fish's head, in the 'shoulder' region of the animal.

GLOSSARY

Plankton Tiny plants and animals that float in the surface of the sea.

Polyp A single coral animal or one of its relatives, such as a sea anemone.

Scales A protective covering of thin slips of bone, usually rounded in shape, arranged like roof tiles over the body of most fishes.

Spawn Fish eggs, or the action of laying eggs.

Spiracle A breathing hole on the top of the head of skates and rays, through which water is taken, uncontaminated by sand or silt from the sea bed.

Streamlined Having a shape that offers least resistance to water or to air, so that an animal can move fast and smoothly.

Swim bladder A balloon-like structure containing gases inside the bodies of most kinds of bony fishes. It acts like an internal lifebuoy and enables the fish to float in the water without effort.

INDEX

aestivation 21, 31
angler fishes 25
anthias 22
archerfish 26

blood 21
bones 12, 28, 30, 31
butterfly fishes 11

camouflage 26
carbon dioxide 8, 31
cartilage 12, 14, 31

covers 7, 31
  filaments 8
  rakers 10, 11, 31
gobies, dwarf 6
grunts, blue-striped 23

hagfishes 7
hatchet fishes,
  freshwater 30
  deep-sea 24
heart 7
herring 19

catfishes 6, 21
cavefishes 30
cichlids 17
clownfishes 23
coelacanths 30
coral polyps 11, 22,
  31

defence 15
denticles 7, 14, 31
dolphins 28
drumming fish 9

eels 18
eggs 16, 17, 19, 31
elvers 18

farm, fish 29
fins 6, 8, 9, 15, 25, 26,
  30, 31
fishing methods 28-29
flying fish 26
food 4, 6, 7, 10, 28,
  29, 31

gills 7, 8, 10, 12, 14,
  15, 20, 21, 31

jaws 7, 10, 11, 25

lampreys 7
lantern fishes 24
larvae 18
lateral line 9, 31
lungfishes 21
lungs 21

marlin 30
migration 18–19
moray eels 11
mouth brooders 17
mudskippers 20

nets 28–29

oarfish 30
Oceans,
  Atlantic 6, 18
  Indian 6, 22
  Pacific 6, 22
oxygen 8, 20, 21, 31

parrot fishes 10
perch, climbing 20
photostomias 24, 25

pike 10
piranhas 27
pitch 9
plankton 6, 14, 31
poison 15, 22, 30
porcupine fishes 27
predators 15, 23, 24,
  27
prey 26
pupfishes, Devil's Hole
  30

rays 7, 14-15, 31
  blond 15
  electric 14
  manta 14
  sting 15
remoras 13
reservoirs 19
rivers 6
roll 9

sailfish 30
salmon 16, 18–19, 28
  ladder 19
scales 6, 7, 31
sea anemones 22, 23,
  31
sea birds 28
seahorses 1, 16
sharks 7, 8, 9, 10, 11,
  12, 14, 17, 29, 31
  basking 11
  eggs 17
  great white 8–9, 12,
  13
  hammerhead 13
  lemon 17
  mako 12
  Port Jackson 17
  sand tiger 12
  tiger 13
  whale 6
  whaler 13
shrimp 11
skates 7, 14-15
skin 7
sound 4, 9, 23
spawn 18–19, 31

spines 15, 21, 22,
  25
spiracles 15
squid 12
sticklebacks 16
stonefish 22
suckers 13
sunfish 17
swim bladder 7, 8, 21,
  31
swimming 6, 8, 12,
  15, 22, 30
swordfish 27, 30

tails 9, 15, 25, 26
teeth 7, 10, 11, 12, 23,
  24
tripod fishes 25
tuna 9, 12, 19, 30
turtles 28

vertebrae 7
viperfishes 24, 25

yaw 9

Photo credits

**Abbreviations: t-top,
m-middle, b-bottom,
r-right, l-left**

Pages 1, 2-3, 10, 11t,
22t, 23b & 29 both –
Frank Spooner
Pictures. 5, 9, 14, 15,
22b & 23t – Linda
Pitkin. 11b, 12 both,
16 & 20 – Bruce
Coleman Collection.
24 & 25 – Planet Earth
Pictures.